CHEERY
UPLIFTING
SHORT STORIES
FOR SENIORS

Engaging, Easy-to-Read Tales Designed to Entertain and Infuse Warm Emotions in the Golden Years, Fostering Joyful Memories and Heartfelt Togetherness

MARGARET RIVERS

TABLE OF CONTENTS

INTRODUCTION

Welcome to " Cheery Uplifting Short Stories for Seniors" by Margaret Rivers—a collection designed to brighten your days, stir your memories, and infuse your heart with positive emotions.

In the golden years of life, where every moment becomes a treasure, the power of positive emotions cannot be understated. Research has shown that cultivating feelings of hope, trust, gratitude, love, serenity, motivation, and enthusiasm can have profound effects on both physical and mental well-being. From boosting immunity to enhancing cognitive function, these emotions serve as the cornerstone of a fulfilling and vibrant life.

This collection is crafted with the recognition of the importance of these emotions in mind. Divided into five sections—each dedicated to exploring one of these powerful sentiments—the stories within these pages aim to uplift, inspire, and rejuvenate.

Through the artistry of Margaret Rivers, each tale is carefully woven to resonate with readers over 70, inviting them to embark on a journey of self-discovery, reflection, and connection. From heartwarming anecdotes to tales of triumph and resilience, these stories offer glimpses into the rich tapestry of human experience, reminding us all of the beauty that surrounds us, even in the simplest of moments.

One of the unique features of this collection is its accessibility. Written in large type, the book is designed to be easily read independently by seniors, allowing them to immerse themselves in the narratives at their own pace. However, it also serves as a wonderful tool for shared enjoyment, fostering moments of bonding and closeness when read aloud to or with loved ones.

The narrative style employed by Margaret Rivers strikes a delicate balance between simplicity and engagement. While the stories are crafted to be easy to understand, they are by no means simplistic or childish. Instead, they offer layers of depth and meaning, inviting readers to explore themes of love, resilience, and the indomitable human spirit.

Furthermore, the varying lengths and complexities of the stories make this collection suitable for seniors of all cognitive abilities. Whether you're seeking a quick pick-me-up or a leisurely read to savor over time, "Uplifting Short Stories for Seniors" offers something for everyone.

As you journey through these pages, may you find solace in the tales of hope, courage, and connection. May you be reminded of the joys of life, the power of human connection, and the resilience of the human spirit. And above all, may you be uplifted, inspired, and filled with an abundance of positive emotions.

So sit back, relax, and prepare to embark on a journey of discovery and delight. With "Uplifting Short Stories for Seniors," every page is an invitation to embrace the beauty of life and celebrate the wisdom that comes with age.

HOPE

Welcome to the section on "Hope" in the collection of "Cheery Uplifting Short Stories for Seniors" by Margaret Rivers—a testament to the enduring power of positive emotions to brighten our lives and uplift our spirits.

In the golden years of life, the importance of hope cannot be understated. It is a beacon of light that guides us through the darkest of nights, a steady hand that leads us towards brighter tomorrows. For seniors in particular, hope is not just a fleeting sentiment; it is a lifeline—a source of comfort, strength, and resilience in the face of life's uncertainties.

In this section, we delve into the theme of hope with a collection of stories that celebrate the human spirit and encounter that changes her life forever, we see the profound impact that hope can have when shared with others.

For seniors over 70, trust often goes hand in hand with hope—a steadfast belief in the goodness of others, in the inherent resilience of the human spirit, and in the promise of better days ahead. In the stories that follow, readers will witness the power of trust to overcome adversity, bridge divides, and forge new beginnings.

As you embark on this journey through the realm of hope, may you be inspired by the resilience of the human spirit, uplifted by the power of possibility, and filled with an abiding sense of optimism for the future. For in the stories of Grandpa John, Evelyn, Clara, and many others, we find echoes of our own hopes and dreams, and a reminder that even in the darkest of times, there is always a glimmer of light to guide us home.

The Unexpected Rescue

Grandpa John and his grandson, Jim, set out for a leisurely stroll through the woods behind their home, the autumn leaves crunching beneath their feet. But what started as a simple walk soon turned into an unexpected adventure.

As they wandered deeper into the woods, the sun began to set, casting long shadows through the trees. Grandpa John glanced at his watch, realizing they had lost track of time. Panic crept into his heart as he realized they were lost.

Jim tried to stay brave, but even his young spirit couldn't mask the worry in his eyes. Grandpa John put on a brave face, reassuring his grandson that everything would be alright.

Hours passed, and darkness descended upon the forest. Just when hope seemed to fade, a distant voice called out their names. Startled, they turned to see their neighbor, Mr. Wilson, emerging from the shadows.

Mr. Wilson, whom they had always considered gruff and distant, now appeared as a beacon of hope in their darkest hour. With a lantern in hand, he guided them back to safety, his gruff exterior softened by the kindness he showed.

As they walked, Grandpa John couldn't help but feel a sense of gratitude and wonder. Sometimes, it takes getting lost to find unexpected kindness in the most unlikely places.

Back home, safe and sound, Grandpa John tucked Jim into bed, the events of the night still fresh in their minds. As they reflected on their adventure, they realized that even in the midst of uncertainty, there is always hope.

The next morning, Grandpa John and Jim visited Mr. Wilson to express their gratitude. Over cups of hot cocoa, they laughed and shared stories, forging a friendship that would last a lifetime.

In the end, their adventure in the woods taught them an important lesson: no matter how lost or frightened we may feel, there is always someone willing to lend a helping hand and guide us back to safety. And with that knowledge, they faced each new day with hope in their hearts, ready to embrace whatever adventures lay ahead.

As the seasons changed and years passed, the memory of their woodland adventure remained etched in their hearts, a testament to the power of hope and the bonds that unite us all. And though time may weather their bodies, the flame of hope within them burned ever brighter, guiding them through life's twists and turns with unwavering certainty.

The Garden of Resilience

In a quiet corner of a small town nestled between rolling hills, there lay a forgotten garden. Its once vibrant flowers had wilted, and its paths were overgrown with weeds. But amidst the neglect, a glimmer of hope remained.

Miss Evelyn, a sprightly woman in her seventies, often passed by the garden on her daily walks. Despite its unkempt appearance, she couldn't shake the feeling that there was something special about it.

One crisp autumn morning, Miss Evelyn decided to venture into the garden. With each step, she felt a sense of anticipation building within her. As she wandered through the maze of vegetation, she discovered small patches of life peeking through the tangled mess—tiny buds fighting to bloom, resilient against the odds.

Moved by the tenacity of these plants, Miss Evelyn resolved to breathe new life into the forgotten garden. She gathered her gardening tools and set to work, pulling weeds, pruning shrubs, and nurturing the struggling flowers back to health.

Word of Miss Evelyn's project spread throughout the town, and soon, neighbors began to lend a hand. Together, they transformed the garden into a vibrant oasis of color and life.

As the seasons changed, so did the garden. Spring brought a riot of blossoms, while summer saw the garden buzzing with the hum of bees and the chirping of birds. In the crisp days of autumn, the trees blazed with fiery hues, and in winter, the garden lay quiet, patiently awaiting the return of spring.

The garden became more than just a place of beauty—it became a symbol of resilience and hope for the entire community. People would come from far and wide to stroll through its winding paths, finding solace and inspiration in its ever-changing landscape.

Years passed, and Miss Evelyn grew older, her steps becoming slower and her hair tinged with gray. But her spirit remained as vibrant as ever, buoyed by the hope she had nurtured in the garden.

One day, as Miss Evelyn sat on a bench in the garden, surrounded by the fruits of her labor, she felt a sense of peace wash over her. She had come to realize that no matter how dark the world may seem, there would always be pockets of beauty and resilience waiting to be discovered.

With a contented sigh, Miss Evelyn closed her eyes, feeling the warmth of the sun on her face and the gentle rustle of leaves in the breeze. In that moment, she knew that as long as there was hope, there would always be a reason to keep moving forward.

Autumn's Embrace:
Clara's Serendipitous Reunion

In a quiet neighborhood nestled between towering trees and cobblestone paths, there lived an elderly woman named Clara. She spent her days tending to her cozy cottage and reminiscing about the memories she had collected over a lifetime.

One brisk autumn morning, as Clara was strolling through the park, she spotted an old friend she hadn't seen in years—Eleanor. Their eyes met, and a spark of recognition ignited between them.

"Clara, is that you?" Eleanor exclaimed, her voice tinged with disbelief and joy.

Clara's heart skipped a beat as she rushed to embrace her long-lost friend. They exchanged stories of their lives since they had last met, sharing laughter and tears as they reminisced about days gone by.

As they sat on a nearby bench, bathed in the warm glow of the afternoon sun, Clara couldn't help but feel a surge of hope coursing through her veins. Here she was, reunited with a dear friend after all this time. It was as if the universe had conspired to bring them together once more.

Over the following weeks, Clara and Eleanor rekindled their friendship, spending hours lost in conversation and laughter. They explored the quaint streets of their neighborhood, discovering hidden treasures and creating new memories along the way.

With each passing day, Clara felt her spirits lift as she embraced the unexpected joy that had entered her life. She realized that even in the twilight years, there was still room for hope and happiness.

As the leaves began to change and the air turned crisp with the promise of winter, Clara and Eleanor made a pact to cherish every moment they had together. For they knew that life was fleeting, but the bonds of friendship were everlasting.

And so, dear reader, let Clara's story serve as a reminder that hope can blossom in the most unexpected places, and that true friendship has the power to light up even the darkest of days.

John's New Journey

In the heart of a bustling city, there stood a quaint little shoe shop owned by an elderly shoemaker named John. For years, John had lovingly crafted shoes for the townsfolk, each pair a testament to his skill and dedication. But as the years passed and John's joints grew stiff with age, he found himself struggling to keep up with the demands of his trade.

With a heavy heart, John made the difficult decision to close his shop. As he turned the sign on the door to "Closed" for the last time, a wave of uncertainty washed over him. What would he do now? Without his beloved shop, would he feel lost and useless?

But John's worries soon melted away as he discovered a new purpose waiting just around the corner. You see, John may have closed his shop, but he was about to embark on the most rewarding journey of his life.

It all started one sunny afternoon when Mrs. Brown, a neighbor from down the street, knocked on John's door with a desperate plea for help. Her regular babysitter had canceled at the last minute, and she had no one to watch her grandchildren while she ran errands.

Without hesitation, John welcomed Mrs. Brown and her grandchildren into his home. As the children giggled and played around him, John felt a warmth spreading through his heart. For the first time in a long time, he felt needed and appreciated.

Word of John's babysitting skills spread like wildfire throughout the block, and soon, he found himself inundated with requests from busy parents in need of a helping hand. With each new babysitting gig, John discovered a newfound sense of purpose and joy.

He delighted in reading bedtime stories to wide-eyed children, teaching them how to tie their shoes, and sharing stories of his days as a shoemaker. And in return, the children showered him with hugs, laughter, and boundless affection.

As the days turned into weeks and the weeks into months, John's reputation as the best-loved babysitter in the block grew. Parents would line up to book his services months in advance, and children would eagerly count down the days until their next playdate with "Uncle John."

And so, in the twilight years of his life, John found hope in the most unexpected of places. No longer did he feel lost or useless. Instead, he felt alive and full of purpose, surrounded by the laughter and love of the children he had come to adore.

As he watched the sun set over the city skyline, John couldn't help but smile. For in the embrace of hope, he had discovered a new chapter of his life—one filled with joy, laughter, and the boundless possibilities of tomorrow.

Catherine's Leap of Hope

In a cozy little house nestled on the corner of Maple Street, there lived an elderly woman named Catherine. At seventy-five, Catherine had lived a life filled with ups and downs, but nothing could have prepared her for the challenge that lay ahead.

It started with a simple misstep—a slip on a patch of ice that sent Catherine tumbling to the ground. In an instant, her world was turned upside down as she felt the sharp pain shoot through her leg. The doctors said it was a bad fall, one that might leave her unable to walk again.

For weeks, Catherine lay in her bed, her body wracked with pain and her spirits sinking lower with each passing day. Even her physiotherapy exercises seemed to offer little solace, as she struggled to find the motivation to keep going.

But in the quiet moments of the evening, as she lay in bed and whispered her prayers to the heavens above,

Catherine clung to a sliver of hope—a tiny flicker of optimism that refused to be extinguished.

Then, one ordinary day, something extraordinary happened. Catherine's daughter had come to visit, and as she stepped into the kitchen to make coffee, her granddaughter Anne toddled into the room, her chubby legs wobbling precariously as she clambered onto the edge of the sofa.

Without a second thought, Catherine sprang into action. With a burst of energy that seemed to come from nowhere, she pushed herself up from her armchair and lunged across the room, catching Anne just as she teetered on the brink of falling.

In that moment, Catherine felt something shift within her—a surge of strength and vitality that she hadn't felt in weeks. As she held her granddaughter in her arms, she realized that she was standing on her own two feet, her legs steady beneath her for the first time in what felt like an eternity.

From that day forward, Catherine's recovery seemed to progress by leaps and bounds. With each passing day, she grew stronger and more determined, her body responding to the newfound hope and optimism that filled her heart.

And as she took her first tentative steps outside, the warm spring sun shining down on her face, Catherine knew that she had experienced a miracle. She had defied the odds and overcome the seemingly insurmountable challenge that lay before her.

The moral of the story, Catherine realized, was simple yet profound: in the darkest of times, when all hope seems lost, it's important to hold onto that tiny glimmer of optimism, for it is often in our darkest moments that miracles happen. And as long as we keep believing, anything is possible.

Peter's Marathon of Hope

In the heart of a bustling city, where the streets pulsed with life and energy, there lived a man named Peter. At seventy years old, Peter had spent a lifetime chasing after dreams and racing against time, but now, as he faced the twilight of his years, he found himself grappling with a new challenge—a failing heart.

Once, Peter had been a runner—a fleet-footed athlete who had glided across finish lines with the grace of a gazelle. But as the years passed, his heart began to betray him, slowing him down and forcing him to take each step with caution.

Still, Peter refused to let his condition define him. Each day, he laced up his running shoes and set out for a light jog, his spirit undaunted by the limitations of his body. And when the opportunity arose to run in a charity marathon, he seized it with both hands, his heart swelling with hope and enthusiasm. But fate had other plans. A visit to the doctor revealed a worsening of Peter's condition—a setback that left him feeling despondent and defeated. How could he run a marathon when his own heart betrayed him?

In the days that followed, Peter found himself adrift in a sea of sadness, his dreams slipping through his fingers like grains of sand. But deep within him, a flicker of hope remained—a tiny spark that refused to be extinguished.

And so, with nothing left to lose, Peter decided to embark on a journey—a journey back to New Orleans, the city where he had once lived and loved, in search of solace and comfort among old friends.

As he wandered the familiar streets, memories came flooding back to him—memories of laughter and camaraderie, of shared dreams and shared struggles. And with each step, Peter felt a renewed sense of purpose and determination stirring within him—a feeling of hope that he thought he had lost forever.

But it wasn't until he reunited with his old colleagues that Peter truly began to believe in the power of hope. As they reminisced about the good old days and shared stories of triumph and defeat, Peter felt a sense of belonging wash over him—a feeling of trust and camaraderie that he hadn't felt in years. And when he returned home, his heart lighter than it had been in months, Peter made a decision. He would not let his condition defeat him. He would not give up on his dreams.

With a newfound sense of determination, Peter sought out a second opinion—a new cardiologist who listened to his story with compassion and understanding. And to Peter's astonishment, the diagnosis was not what he expected.

His heart, once deemed a liability, was now strong and healthy—a testament to the power of hope and resilience. And as he laced up his running shoes once more, Peter felt a sense of gratitude wash over him—a gratitude for the journey that had brought him to this moment, and the trust and hope that had carried him through.

For Peter knew that anything was possible when hope and confidence overcame sadness and despondency. And as he crossed the finish line of the marathon, his heart pounding with joy and exhilaration, he knew that he had triumphed against all odds.

GRATITUDE

Welcome to the section on "Gratitude" in the collection of " Cheery Uplifting Short Stories for Seniors " by Margaret Rivers—a celebration of the transformative power of appreciation and thankfulness in our lives.

Gratitude is a timeless virtue that transcends age, culture, and circumstance—a source of solace, strength, and joy for people of all walks of life. For the elderly, in particular, gratitude takes on a profound significance, serving as a guiding light through the journey of aging and offering a pathway to greater well-being and fulfillment.

In this section, we explore the theme of gratitude through a collection of stories that illuminate the beauty and richness of a thankful heart. Through the skillful storytelling of Margaret Rivers, readers are invited to embark on a journey of reflection, inspiration, and gratitude.

Gratitude, as research has shown, is more than just a fleeting emotion—it is a powerful force that has the potential to transform our physical and mental well-being. Scientific studies have linked the practice of gratitude to numerous health benefits, including improved immune function, reduced stress levels, and enhanced overall happiness. By cultivating an attitude of gratitude, we can cultivate a deeper sense of contentment and peace in our lives.

In the stories that follow, readers will encounter a diverse cast of characters who embody the spirit of gratitude in its many forms. From Lester the cat, to Anthony's passion for painting, whose simple acts of gratitude sparks a chain reaction of joy and generosity, each story serves as a reminder of the profound impact that gratitude can have on our lives.

But perhaps most touching of all are the stories of Alex's sweetness towards his grandmother—a testament to the enduring bond of love and gratitude between generations. In the small acts of kindness and appreciation that Alex shows towards his grandmother, we see the transformative power of gratitude to strengthen relationships, foster connection, and bring joy to both giver and receiver.

For the elderly, in particular, the practice of gratitude takes on added significance as a means of finding meaning and purpose. As we reflect on the blessings and abundance that surround us, we are reminded of the countless gifts that life has bestowed upon us, from the simple pleasures of nature to the love and support of family and friends.

As you journey through the stories in this section, may you be inspired to cultivate a spirit of gratitude in your own life.

May you find joy in the small moments of kindness and beauty that fill your days, and may you be reminded of the countless reasons we have to be thankful, even in the face of adversity.

With each tale, may you be uplifted, inspired, and filled with an abiding sense of gratitude for the richness and beauty of life. For in the practice of gratitude, we find not only a source of strength and resilience, but also a pathway to greater peace, contentment, and joy.

Lester's Legacy of Gratitude

In a quaint little town nestled between the mountains, there lived a wise old cat named Lester. Lester wasn't your ordinary feline—he had a special gift for spreading gratitude wherever he went.

Every morning, Lester would venture out into the neighborhood, his sleek black fur shining in the sunlight. He would visit the homes of the townsfolk, greeting them with a gentle purr and a nudge of his head.

Lester's first stop was always Mrs. Robbins' house. Mrs. Robbins was a widow who lived alone, and Lester knew just how much she cherished his company. He would curl up in her lap, his soothing purrs bringing her comfort and joy.

Next, Lester would make his way to Mr. Thompson's bakery. Mr. Thompson was a gruff old man with a heart of gold, and he always had a special treat waiting for Lester— a freshly baked fish pie just for him. In return, Lester would grace Mr. Thompson's shop with his presence, attracting customers with his friendly demeanor.

As the day wore on, Lester would continue his rounds, spreading gratitude wherever he went. He would visit the local nursing home, bringing smiles to the faces of the residents with his playful antics. He would patrol the streets, keeping a watchful eye on the neighborhood and chasing away any pesky mice that dared to cause trouble.

But Lester's true gift lay in his ability to teach others the power of gratitude. He showed them that even in the darkest of times, there was always something to be thankful for—a warm bed to sleep in, a delicious meal to eat, the companionship of loved ones.

One day, as Lester made his rounds, he stumbled upon a lost kitten wandering the streets. The kitten was cold, hungry, and afraid, but Lester took her under his wing, showing her kindness and compassion.

As the years passed, Lester's legacy of gratitude continued to grow.

Inspired by Lester's example, the city decided to honor him by opening a home for abandoned cats, naming it "Lester's Haven." It became a sanctuary where cats could find love, care, and companionship, just as Lester had provided for so many during his time in the town. And as the years passed, Lester's legacy of gratitude continued to inspire hope and kindness in the hearts of all who knew his story.

The Colorful Adventures of Anthony

Meet Anthony, an 81-year-old man with a zest for life and a passion for painting. For years, Anthony had delighted in capturing the beauty of the world on canvas, until cataracts clouded his vision and robbed him of his ability to see the vibrant colors that once filled his days.

But one fateful day, Anthony decided enough was enough. He marched into the eye doctor's office with determination in his heart and a twinkle in his eye, ready to tackle his cataracts head-on.

As he sat in the waiting room, Anthony couldn't help but feel a flutter of excitement in his chest. Soon, he would once again be able to see the world in all its colorful glory—a prospect that filled him with gratitude and anticipation.

Finally, the moment arrived. Anthony was wheeled into the operating room, where the skilled surgeon worked their magic to remove the cataracts that had clouded his vision for far too long.

When Anthony awoke from the anesthesia, he blinked his eyes in wonder, marveling at the newfound clarity of his vision. Colors seemed brighter, more vibrant, as if the world had suddenly come alive before his very eyes. With a grin stretching from ear to ear, Anthony wasted no time in putting his restored vision to good use. He dusted off his old paintbrushes, squeezed out tubes of colorful paint, and set to work on his latest masterpiece—a breathtaking landscape that captured the beauty of the world in all its glory.

But Anthony's adventures didn't stop there. With his newfound clarity of vision, he decided to indulge in another passion he had long neglected—driving. With the wind in his hair and a smile on his face, Anthony hit the open road, relishing in the freedom and independence that came with being behind the wheel once again.

As he cruised along the winding country roads, Anthony couldn't help but feel a profound sense of gratitude for the simple pleasures of life—the vibrant colors of nature, the thrill of the open road, and the joy of pursuing his passions without limitation.

And so, dear reader, let Anthony's story serve as a reminder that gratitude can be found in the most unexpected of places. Whether it's the beauty of a colorful landscape, the freedom of the open road, or the simple joy of pursuing our passions, there is always something to be thankful for in this wonderful journey called life.

The Misadventures of Elizabeth and Tony

Once upon a time, in a cozy little neighborhood, there lived a spunky senior named Elizabeth and her mischievous red cat, Tony. Now, Tony had a knack for getting into all sorts of trouble, much to Elizabeth's chagrin. But despite his antics, she loved him dearly and couldn't imagine life without him.

One sunny afternoon, as Elizabeth was puttering around the house, she realized with a sinking feeling in her stomach that Tony was nowhere to be found. She searched high and low, calling out his name and shaking his favorite treats, but there was no sign of the little troublemaker.

With a heavy heart, Elizabeth ventured out into the neighborhood, asking her neighbors if they had seen Tony anywhere. But alas, no one had spotted the elusive red cat.

As the hours stretched into days, Elizabeth began to fear the worst. She plastered the neighborhood with posters and searched every nook and cranny, but Tony remained stubbornly out of sight.

Just when Elizabeth was beginning to lose hope, a glimmer of excitement sparked in her eyes. Two days after Tony had disappeared, she decided to take a trip to the supermarket to stock up on groceries.

As she pushed her cart down the aisles, tossing cans of cat food and bags of treats into her basket, Elizabeth couldn't shake the feeling that she was being watched. She glanced around, her eyes scanning the crowded store until they landed on the most unexpected sight. There, perched precariously atop a towering display of canned goods, was none other than Tony himself! His fluffy red fur stood out like a beacon among the sea of products, and his mischievous green eyes twinkled with amusement as he surveyed his surroundings.

"Tony, you little rascal!" Elizabeth exclaimed, a mixture of relief and exasperation flooding through her. "What on earth are you doing up there?"

But Tony merely flicked his tail in response, as if to say, "What does it look like? I'm on a grand adventure, of course!"

With a sigh and a shake of her head, Elizabeth carefully plucked Tony from his perch and cradled him in her arms. She couldn't help but feel a surge of gratitude for the mischievous little cat who had managed to brighten her day with his unexpected antics.

As they made their way to the checkout counter, Elizabeth couldn't stop chuckling at the absurdity of the situation. Who would have thought that she would find her beloved Tony inside the supermarket of all places?

And as they walked home together, Elizabeth couldn't help but feel a renewed sense of gratitude for the furry companion who had a knack for turning even the most mundane of errands into an adventure to remember. After all, life with Tony was never dull, and for that, Elizabeth was truly grateful.

A Garden of Gratitude

Mr. Bernard had lived a solitary life for as long as he could remember. His days were spent tending to his beloved garden of white roses, finding solace in their delicate beauty and quiet company.

One crisp morning, as Mr. Bernard stepped into his garden, he was greeted not by the serene sight of his beloved roses, but by a tangled mess of string and fabric. A kite, it seemed, had crashed into his precious flowers, leaving behind a trail of destruction.

Mr. Bernard's initial reaction was one of fury. How dare someone disrupt his carefully cultivated sanctuary! With each tug and pull to free the kite from his roses, his frustration grew until he was practically fuming. But just as he was about to unleash a torrent of angry words, a voice interrupted his thoughts.

"Excuse me, sir, I'm so sorry about the kite. It was my son's, Tom. He didn't mean any harm, I promise."

Mr. Bernard turned to see a woman standing at the edge of his garden, her eyes filled with concern. He braced himself for a confrontation, ready to unleash his pent-up anger.

But as he looked into the woman's eyes, something shifted within him. He saw not a trespasser, but a mother filled with worry for her child. And in that moment, Mr. Bernard felt a twinge of compassion stirring in his heart.

He softened his gaze and took a deep breath, willing himself to let go of his anger.

"It's alright," he said, his voice surprisingly gentle. "Accidents happen."

The woman's face lit up with relief, and she hurried over to help disentangle the kite from the roses. As they worked side by side, Mr. Bernard couldn't help but notice the warmth of her smile and the kindness in her eyes.

After the kite was finally freed, the woman introduced herself as Rose, and her son, Tom. They chatted amiably for a while, exchanging stories and laughter amidst the fragrant blooms of the garden.

In the days that followed, Rose and Tom became frequent visitors to Mr. Bernard's garden. They brought with them a sense of joy and companionship that had long been missing from his life.

Rose, with her gentle demeanor and compassionate spirit, reminded Mr. Bernard of the daughter he had never had. And Tom, with his infectious laughter and boundless energy, filled the garden with the playful chatter of a grandchild.

As the seasons changed and the roses bloomed anew, Mr. Bernard found himself overwhelmed with gratitude for the unexpected gift of friendship. He realized that sometimes, out of the most unlikely circumstances, the most beautiful relationships can blossom.

And so, in the midst of his garden of white roses, Mr. Bernard discovered that gratitude could be found not only in the flowers that bloomed, but in the hearts of those who tended to them with love.

Alex's Gratitude Mission

In a quiet neighborhood, Grandma Rose sat on her porch, her brow furrowed with worry. She had been trying to solve a problem for days, but no solution seemed to present itself. Her thoughts were interrupted by the sound of the front door opening, and in stepped her 12-year-old grandson, Alex.

"Hey, Grandma! I'm here for the weekend," Alex exclaimed, his eyes bright with excitement.

Grandma Rose smiled warmly at her grandson, grateful for his cheerful presence. Little did she know, Alex would soon become her unlikely hero.

As the weekend unfolded, Grandma Rose found herself confiding in Alex about her worries. She explained how she had gotten into an argument with Mrs. Jenkins, their sweet old neighbor, over the condominium expenses— a disagreement that had left her feeling frustrated and upset.

Alex listened intently, his young mind whirring with ideas. He knew he had to do something to help his grandmother find peace and resolution.

The next morning, Alex set his plan into motion. Armed with construction paper, markers, and a whole lot of creativity, he disappeared into the kitchen, leaving Grandma Rose curious about his antics.

After a few hours of silence, Alex emerged with a colorful poster in hand—a masterpiece that would soon melt Grandma Rose's heart and fill Mrs. Miller with gratitude.

"Grandma, come outside! I have something to show you," Alex called out, his excitement contagious.

Curious, Grandma Rose followed Alex to the front yard, where he had set up a makeshift display. On the poster, in big bold letters, were the words: "Thank You, Mrs. Miller!"

Below the words were dozens of colorful handprints, each one representing a member of the neighborhood. Alex had gone door to door, collecting handprints from every resident, young and old, to create a beautiful collage of gratitude for Mrs. Miller.

As Mrs. Miller stepped out of her house, she was greeted with the sight of the colorful poster and the smiling faces of her neighbors. Tears welled up in her eyes as she read the heartfelt messages of thanks and appreciation.

"Alex, what is all this?" Grandma Rose asked, her heart swelling with pride for her grandson's thoughtful gesture.

"I wanted to show Mrs. Miller how much we appreciate her, Grandma. Even though you had an argument, I know deep down you still care about her," Alex explained, his eyes shining with sincerity.

Grandma Rose couldn't help but feel a surge of gratitude for her clever grandson. In his own unique way, Alex had helped her reconcile with Mrs. Miller and mend their fractured relationship.

As Mrs. Miller wiped away her tears and embraced her neighbors, Grandma Rose realized just how lucky she was to have Alex by her side. His kindness, creativity, and unwavering love had filled her heart with gratitude and reminded her of the power of forgiveness and reconciliation.

And as the neighborhood came together to celebrate their sweet old neighbor, Grandma Rose couldn't help but feel a profound sense of gratitude for the wonderful community she called home—and for her incredible grandson, whose love and compassion knew no bounds.

Seeds of Kindness: Adam's Abundance Garden

In a quiet corner of the town where the streets seemed to echo with the whispers of days gone by, there lived a retired plumber named Adam. At seventy-eight, Adam had spent a lifetime fixing leaky pipes and unclogging drains, but now, in his golden years, he found himself feeling lonely and adrift, the once-familiar rhythms of his life fading into the background.

But one day, everything changed. Adam's neighbors, touched by his quiet kindness and gentle demeanor, came together to offer him a gift—a piece of land where he could fulfill his dream of starting a vegetable garden.

At first, Adam was hesitant. Farming was a far cry from fixing pipes, and he wasn't sure if he had the green thumb required to make the garden thrive. But with a heart full of gratitude and a newfound sense of purpose, he decided to give it a try.

With each passing day, Adam poured his heart and soul into the garden, tending to the soil with care and attention. And as the first shoots of green began to poke through the earth, he felt a sense of joy and satisfaction unlike anything he had ever experienced before.

But it wasn't just the act of gardening that filled Adam with gratitude—it was the kindness of his neighbors, who had given him the gift of hope and purpose in his darkest hour. And so, with a heart full of gratitude, Adam set out to share his newfound joy with the world.

As the vegetables began to ripen on the vine, Adam found himself with more than he could possibly eat on his own. And so, he decided to share his bounty with his neighbors, leaving baskets of fresh produce on their doorsteps with a note of thanks.

The response was overwhelming. Adam's neighbors, touched by his generosity, began to return the favor in kind, bringing him homemade pies and jars of preserves in exchange for his fresh vegetables.

And so, a beautiful cycle of gratitude was born. Each day, Adam's garden became a joyful meeting place for the whole neighborhood, where young and old alike would come together to share stories, laughter, and, of course, delicious food.

But perhaps the greatest gift of all was the sense of community that blossomed in the shadow of Adam's garden. What had once been a lonely corner of the town was now alive with the sounds of friendship and laughter, thanks to Adam's selfless act of gratitude.

As the seasons turned and the years passed, Adam's garden continued to thrive, a testament to the power of gratitude and the joy that comes from giving back to others. And as he looked out over his lush green oasis, surrounded by friends and loved ones, Adam knew that he had found true happiness at last—thanks to the simple act of planting a seed of gratitude in his heart.

MOTIVATION

Welcome to the section on "Motivation" in the collection of " Cheery Uplifting Short Stories for Seniors " by Margaret Rivers—a journey into the boundless reservoir of strength, resilience, and enthusiasm that resides within each and every one of us, regardless of age.

As we navigate the winding paths of life, the importance of motivation and enthusiasm becomes increasingly apparent. For the elderly, in particular, these emotions serve as vital pillars of support, empowering us to face the challenges of aging with courage, determination, and optimism.

In this section, we explore the theme of motivation through a series of inspiring stories that celebrate the indomitable human spirit and the power of a positive mindset. Through Margaret Rivers' poignant storytelling, readers are invited to embark on a journey of self-discovery, empowerment, and renewed purpose.

Motivation is more than just a fleeting feeling; it is a driving force that propels us forward, even in the face of adversity. It is the spark that ignites our passions, the fuel that sustains our dreams, and the guiding light that leads us towards our goals. In the stories that follow, readers will encounter a diverse cast of characters who embody the spirit of motivation in its many forms.

From the courageous acts of the elderly fireman Bob to the adventures of George and his beloved motorbike, each story serves as a testament to the transformative power of motivation and enthusiasm.

But perhaps most inspiring of all are the stories of Kate, the retired schoolteacher, whose unwavering commitment to her students and passion for learning ignites a spark of curiosity and enthusiasm in the hearts of all who encounter her. In the faces of her new pupils, she finds renewed purpose and meaning, reminding us that age is no barrier to the pursuit of knowledge and growth.

For the elderly, maintaining a sense of motivation and enthusiasm is crucial not only for physical and mental well-being but also for overall quality of life. It is a reminder that no matter how old we may be, there is always something new to learn, explore, and experience.

As you journey through the stories in this section, may you be inspired to cultivate a spirit of motivation and enthusiasm in your own life. May you embrace each day with renewed vigor and zest, and may you discover the joy and fulfillment that comes from pursuing your passions and dreams, no matter your age.

With each tale, may you be uplifted, inspired, and filled with an abiding sense of motivation to embrace life's challenges and opportunities with open arms. For in the practice of motivation and enthusiasm, we find not only the key to a fulfilling and meaningful life, but also the courage to face whatever may come our way, with grace and determination.

Bob's Beacon of Hope

In a small town where the sun seemed to always shine a little brighter, there lived an old fireman named Bob. At seventy-five, his weathered hands and silvered hair told tales of a lifetime spent in service to others. But retirement hadn't dulled his spirit; if anything, it burned even brighter with each passing day.

Despite hanging up his helmet years ago, Bob found himself longing for the camaraderie and sense of purpose that came with being a firefighter. So, one brisk morning, he decided to pay a visit to the local fire station, his heart brimming with enthusiasm and determination.

As he stepped through the familiar doors, memories flooded back to him—the sound of alarms blaring, the rush of adrenaline as they raced to save lives. But it was the sense of community that he missed the most—the shared sense of purpose that bound them together like family.

To his surprise, the current firefighters welcomed him with open arms, eager to hear tales of his firefighting days and learn from his wealth of experience. Bob's enthusiasm was contagious, reigniting a spark within the station that had dimmed in his absence.

Before long, Bob found himself back in action, albeit in a different capacity. No longer wielding a hose or scaling ladders, he served as a mentor to the younger firefighters, his wisdom guiding them through even the toughest of challenges.

But Bob's impact extended far beyond the walls of the fire station. His presence served as a beacon of hope to the entire town, reminding them that age was just a number and that passion knew no bounds.

On sunny days, Bob could be found leading fire safety workshops for local schools, his eyes alight with excitement as he shared his knowledge with eager young minds. And on stormy nights, he stood alongside his fellow firefighters, a steady hand in the face of adversity.

Through it all, Bob never lost his zest for life or his unwavering commitment to serving others. His story served as a reminder that no matter how old we grow, there's always room for new adventures and opportunities to make a difference.

The Soup Kitchen Samaritan

In the heart of the bustling city, where the hustle and bustle seemed to drown out the echoes of kindness, there lived an elderly woman named Margaret. At seventy-eight, her days were spent in quiet solitude, but her heart yearned for something more—a chance to make a difference in the lives of others.

One chilly morning, Margaret stumbled upon a bustling soup kitchen tucked away in a nondescript alley. Intrigued by the sense of purpose that emanated from within, she stepped inside, her curiosity piqued and her spirits lifted.

As she watched the volunteers bustle about, serving hot meals to those in need, Margaret felt a spark ignite within her—a newfound sense of motivation and enthusiasm that she hadn't felt in years.

Without hesitation, Margaret rolled up her sleeves and joined the ranks of the volunteers, her hands eager to lend a helping hand. With each bowl of soup she ladled and every smile she shared, her sense of fulfillment grew, filling the void that had long lingered within her soul.

But it wasn't just the act of serving meals that brought Margaret joy; it was the connections she forged with those she served. In their eyes, she saw stories of struggle and resilience, of hope amidst hardship. And in their gratitude, she found a sense of purpose that she had been searching for all along.

Weeks turned into months, and Margaret became a familiar face at the soup kitchen, her enthusiasm never waning. She shared laughter and tears with her fellow volunteers, forming bonds that transcended age and circumstance.

And as she looked around the bustling soup kitchen, Margaret realized that she wasn't just serving meals— she was serving hope. Each bowl of soup was a symbol of compassion and kindness, a reminder that even in the darkest of times, there was still goodness to be found.

In the twilight of her years, Margaret had discovered that true motivation wasn't found in accolades or achievements, but in the simple act of giving back. And as she left the soup kitchen that evening, her heart full and her spirits soaring, she knew that she had found her purpose—a purpose rooted in love, kindness, and the unwavering belief that even the smallest gestures could make the biggest difference.

And so, in the golden years of his life, Bob continued to inspire those around him, proving that with a heart full of passion and a spirit that refused to be extinguished, anything was possible. Inspired by Lester's example, the city decided to honor him by opening a home for abandoned cats, naming it "Lester's Haven." It became a sanctuary where cats could find love, care, and companionship, just as Lester had provided for so many during his time in the town.

And as the years passed, Lester's legacy of gratitude continued to inspire hope and kindness in the hearts of all who knew his story.

The Ride of Renewal

In a sleepy town where time seemed to linger in the air like a familiar melody, there lived an elderly man named George. At seventy-two, his days were spent reminiscing about the adventures of his youth, his eyes twinkling with the memories of days gone by.

But as the years passed, George found himself longing for a new adventure, a chance to reignite the fire that once burned within him. And so, one crisp autumn morning, he dusted off his old motorbike—a relic from a time long past—and set out on a journey to rediscover the thrill of the open road.

As he revved the engine, the familiar rumble echoed through the streets, stirring something deep within George's soul. With each twist of the throttle, he felt a sense of freedom wash over him—a renewed sense of purpose that had long eluded him.

Through winding country roads and sprawling fields of gold, George rode with a sense of determination, his spirit soaring with each passing mile. The wind whipped through his hair, carrying with it the promise of new beginnings and endless possibilities.

But it wasn't just the thrill of the ride that filled George with enthusiasm—it was the sights and sounds of the world around him. He marveled at the beauty of nature, the vibrant colors of the changing leaves, and the symphony of birdsong that filled the air.

As he stopped to admire a picturesque sunset, George realized that age was just a number, and that the spirit of adventure knew no bounds. With each passing year, he vowed to embrace life with the same zeal and passion that he had in his youth.

And so, as the sun dipped below the horizon, George made a silent promise to himself—to never stop chasing his dreams, to never stop seeking out new adventures, and to never let age define what he was capable of achieving.

For in the seat of his old motorbike, George had found more than just a means of transportation—he had found a symbol of renewal, a reminder that no matter how old we grow, the road ahead is always ripe with opportunity and possibility. And with a heart full of hope and a throttle full of determination, he rode off into the sunset, eager to embrace whatever adventures lay ahead.

From Spatulas to Brushes: The Tale of Chef Claude

Once upon a time, in a bustling town where the aroma of freshly baked bread wafted through the streets, there lived an old cook named Claude. For decades, Claude had wielded his spatula with flair, delighting the townsfolk with his culinary creations at the local diner.

But one fateful day, as Claude flipped pancakes with his usual gusto, he felt a spark of inspiration ignite within him. It was as if a voice whispered in his ear, urging him to explore a new passion beyond the kitchen.

With newfound determination, Claude hung up his apron and traded his spatula for a set of paintbrushes. At first, the townsfolk scoffed at the idea of a cook turning painter, but Claude paid no mind. He was on a mission to unleash his inner artist, and nothing could stand in his way.

Armed with pots of vibrant paint and a canvas as blank as a freshly baked pie crust, Claude set to work. With each stroke of his brush, he poured his heart and soul onto the canvas, creating masterpieces that captured the beauty of the world around him.

As word of Claude's artistic talent spread, the townsfolk flocked to his humble studio, eager to witness the transformation of the old cook into a revered painter. They marveled at the vivid colors and intricate details of his work, unable to believe that the same hands that once wielded a spatula with precision now danced across the canvas with such grace.

But Claude's journey was not without its challenges. There were days when doubt crept in, whispering that he was too old to start anew, too set in his ways to embrace change. Yet, with each setback, Claude summoned the same determination that had fueled his culinary prowess for so many years.

And so, with paint-stained hands and a heart full of passion, Claude persevered. He painted sunsets that set the sky ablaze with fiery hues, landscapes that transported viewers to distant lands, and portraits that captured the essence of the human spirit.

Before long, Claude's paintings adorned the walls of galleries far and wide, earning him acclaim as one of the most talented artists of his generation. But for Claude, the true reward lay not in the accolades, but in the joy of pursuing his passion and inspiring others to do the same.

As the sun dipped below the horizon, casting a golden glow over the town, Claude stood in his studio, surrounded by his paintings and the laughter of friends. And in that moment, he knew that no matter where life's journey may lead, as long as he followed his heart, the possibilities were endless.

A New Chapter Awaits

In a small town where the sun painted the sky in hues of gold and amber, there lived a beloved schoolteacher named Kate. At sixty-eight, Kate had spent a lifetime shaping young minds and nurturing the next generation, but as retirement loomed on the horizon, she found herself filled with a sense of sadness and uncertainty.

For years, Kate had poured her heart and soul into her work, guiding her students with wisdom and compassion. But now, faced with the prospect of leaving behind the only career she had ever known, she couldn't help but feel a twinge of sadness at the thought of saying goodbye.

But then, one day, everything changed. A chance encounter with a group of hospitalized children sparked something within Kate—a newfound sense of purpose and enthusiasm that she hadn't felt in years.

As she sat by their bedsides, reading stories and teaching lessons, Kate felt a warmth spread through her chest—a sense of joy and fulfillment unlike anything she had ever experienced before. For in the faces of those brave young souls, she saw hope and resilience, and she knew that she had found her calling.

From that day forward, Kate threw herself into her work with renewed energy and determination. She spent her days visiting hospitals and hospices, bringing light and laughter to the lives of sick and injured children who needed it most.

And as she watched their faces light up with joy at the sight of her, Kate felt a sense of gratitude wash over her—a gratitude for the opportunity to make a difference in the lives of others, even as her own career drew to a close.

As the end of the school year approached, Kate found herself counting down the days until her retirement with a sense of anticipation rather than sadness. For she knew that with each passing day, she was one step closer to embarking on a new adventure—a chapter filled with purpose and meaning.

And so, when the day finally arrived, and Kate bid farewell to her colleagues and students with tears in her eyes and a smile on her lips, she did so with a heart full of gratitude and excitement for the journey that lay ahead.

For Kate had come to realize that every ending is also a beautiful new beginning—a chance to reinvent oneself and pursue new passions. And as she walked out of the school for the last time, her head held high and her heart full of hope, she knew that the best was yet to come.

The Grateful Builder

In a quiet neighborhood where the trees whispered secrets to the wind, there lived an engineer named Matthew. At seventy-two, Matthew had spent his life designing structures and solving complex problems, but as retirement approached, he found himself feeling adrift, unsure of what the future held.

One stormy afternoon, as dark clouds gathered on the horizon and thunder rumbled in the distance, Matthew's world was turned upside down by a sudden hailstorm. When the skies cleared and the sun emerged once more, Matthew ventured outside to assess the damage, only to find his beloved doghouse in ruins.

At first, anger flared within Matthew's chest. How could this happen? How could such a destructive force wreak havoc on his carefully crafted creation? But as he surveyed the wreckage, a spark of inspiration ignited within him—a newfound passion for building.

With hammer in hand and determination in his heart, Matthew set to work rebuilding the doghouse from the ground up. Each nail hammered into place, each board carefully measured and cut, brought him a sense of purpose and satisfaction unlike anything he had ever experienced before.

And as the days turned into weeks and the weeks turned into months, Matthew's passion for building grew stronger with each passing day. No longer bound by the constraints of his career, he found himself exploring new techniques and pushing the boundaries of his creativity.

But it wasn't just the act of building that filled Matthew with gratitude—it was the storm itself, and the unexpected opportunity it had presented him with. For in the wake of destruction, he had found a new calling—a purpose that filled him with joy and fulfillment.

As he put the finishing touches on the doghouse, Matthew couldn't help but feel a sense of gratitude wash over him—a gratitude for the storm that had torn his world apart and the opportunity it had given him to rebuild it stronger than ever before.

And as he watched his faithful companion, Max, settle into his new home with a contented sigh, Matthew knew that he had found something truly special. For in the midst of chaos and destruction, he had discovered a passion that would bring him joy for years to come.

As he looked out over the horizon, where the clouds gathered once more in a tumultuous dance, Matthew felt a sense of peace settle over him. For he knew that no matter what challenges lay ahead, he would face them with gratitude in his heart, knowing that even the darkest storms can lead to the brightest of blessings.

LOVE

Welcome to the enchanting world of "Love" in the collection of "Cheery Uplifting Short Stories for Seniors" by Margaret Rivers—a treasure trove of heartwarming stories that celebrate the enduring power and beauty of love in all its forms.

Love, often described as the most profound of human emotions, holds a special place in the hearts of people of all ages. For seniors over 70, in particular, love serves as a guiding light, illuminating their lives with warmth, joy, and a deep sense of connection to the world around them.

In this section, we embark on a journey through the multifaceted landscape of love, exploring its myriad expressions and manifestations. From the tender bonds of familial love to the cherished companionship of friends, from the unbreakable bond between humans and their beloved pets to the awe-inspiring beauty of nature, each story offers a glimpse into the transformative power of love.

At the heart of this section lies the essence of romantic love—the timeless tale of Massimiliano, a true story that unfolded on the rails of Italy's iconic train system. Decades after a chance encounter on a train, Massimiliano finds himself once again aboard the same mode of transport, only to be greeted by a remarkable surprise that reignites the flames of love and destiny.

But beyond romantic love, the stories within this section celebrate love in its purest and most universal form—a boundless force that transcends barriers of age, distance, and circumstance. Through Margaret Rivers' evocative storytelling, readers are invited to rediscover the joy of loving and being loved, regardless of where life's journey may lead.

In each tale, we encounter characters who embody the transformative power of love—a grandmother's unwavering devotion to her grandchildren, a friend's selfless act of kindness, a stranger's unexpected gesture of compassion. These stories serve as poignant reminders that love knows no bounds and that even the smallest acts of kindness have the power to ripple through the lives of others, leaving an indelible mark on the heart.

As you immerse yourself in the stories within this section, may you be reminded of the preciousness of love in all its forms. May you find solace in the warmth of familial bonds, inspiration in the beauty of nature, and comfort in the knowledge that love, in its infinite wisdom, has the power to heal, to uplift, and to unite us all.

With each turn of the page, may you be reminded that love is not merely an emotion, but a force of nature—a guiding light that illuminates our path and fills our hearts with hope, joy, and the promise of brighter days ahead. For in the embrace of love, we find the true essence of what it means to be alive—to cherish, to connect, and to celebrate the beauty of the human experience, one story at a time.

Love at the Doctor's Office

At 82 years old, Grace had thought her days of romance were long behind her. Widowed for over a decade, she had grown accustomed to the quiet rhythm of her days, filled with memories of a love that had once filled her heart.

But one fateful day, as Grace sat in the crowded waiting room of her doctor's office, fate decided to intervene in the most unexpected of ways.

As she leafed through a magazine, her attention was suddenly drawn to a kindly gentleman sitting across from her. His warm smile and twinkling eyes seemed to beckon her, stirring something deep within her heart.

Without hesitation, Grace struck up a conversation with the gentleman, whose name turned out to be Harold. They quickly discovered a shared love of classic literature and crossword puzzles, and before they knew it, the waiting room buzzed with laughter and camaraderie.

As they chatted, Grace couldn't help but feel a flutter of excitement in her chest. Could it be that love had found her once again, in the most unexpected of places?

When their names were finally called, Grace and Harold reluctantly bid each other farewell, promising to meet again soon. And true to their word, they began to schedule their doctor's appointments on the same day, eager for the chance to reunite once more.

With each passing visit, Grace and Harold's bond grew stronger, fueled by their shared interests and zest for life. They explored the city together, hand in hand, embarking on adventures neither of them had ever dreamed possible.

From picnics in the park to spontaneous road trips, Grace and Harold's love blossomed like a flower in the springtime, filling their hearts with joy and gratitude.

And on a beautiful summer's day, surrounded by their friends and loved ones, Grace and Harold exchanged vows in a simple yet heartfelt ceremony. It was a celebration of love that had endured the test of time, proving that it's never too late to find happiness in the arms of another.

As they danced beneath the stars, Grace couldn't help but marvel at the unexpected journey that had led her to this moment. For in the waiting room of a doctor's office, she had found not only a husband but a kindred spirit—a love that would light up the rest of her days with laughter, adventure, and endless joy.

And so, dear reader, let Grace and Harold's story serve as a reminder that love knows no bounds, and that it's never too late to open your heart to the possibility of new beginnings.

Kiwi's Canine Comedy

In a cozy little cottage at the edge of town, there lived an elderly couple named Harold and Mildred. Their days were filled with simple pleasures, but the true joy in their lives came from their beloved dog, Kiwi.

Kiwi was a small, scrappy terrier with a heart of gold and a penchant for mischief. From the moment he bounded into their lives, Harold and Mildred knew they were in for an adventure.

One sunny morning, as Harold sat in his favorite armchair sipping his morning tea, Kiwi bounded into the room, a mischievous twinkle in his eye.

"Morning, Kiwi!" Harold chuckled, ruffling the dog's fluffy fur. "What antics do you have planned for us today?"

Kiwi's response was a playful bark, as if to say, "Just wait and see!"

Sure enough, as Mildred stepped into the kitchen to prepare breakfast, she was greeted by the sight of Kiwi standing on his hind legs, attempting to reach a treat jar on the counter.

"Oh, you little rascal!" Mildred laughed, scooping Kiwi up into her arms. "You know you're not supposed to be up there."

But Kiwi merely wagged his tail, his eyes sparkling with mischief.

As the day went on, Kiwi's antics only grew more outrageous. He chased his tail in circles until he collapsed in a dizzy heap, he barked at passing birds with such enthusiasm that they took flight in a flurry of feathers, and he even managed to swipe a slice of cake off the dining table when Mildred wasn't looking.

Through it all, Harold and Mildred couldn't help but laugh at their furry friend's antics. Kiwi brought so much joy and laughter into their lives, and they were grateful for every moment they shared with him.

But amidst all the laughter, there was a deep love that bound Harold, Mildred, and Kiwi together. It was a love that transcended words, a love that could be felt in the wag of a tail, the lick of a tongue, the warmth of a snuggle.

As the sun dipped below the horizon and the stars twinkled overhead, Harold, Mildred, and Kiwi curled up together by the fireplace, basking in the warmth of each other's company.

In that moment, surrounded by love and laughter, they knew that no matter what adventures tomorrow may bring, as long as they had each other, they could weather any storm with a smile on their faces and love in their hearts.

Scott's Garden of Love

In a quaint little town nestled amidst rolling hills and blooming meadows, there lived a retired gardener named Scott. Despite his old age, Scott's love for gardening never waned, and he spent his days tending to his beloved garden with unwavering passion.

One sunny morning, as Scott pottered among his flower beds, he heard a cheerful voice call out from over the fence. It was Mrs. Jenkins, his nosy but well-meaning neighbor, who always seemed to have a knack for poking her nose where it didn't belong.

"Morning, Scott!" Mrs. Jenkins chirped, her voice carrying over the gentle rustle of leaves. "Got any secrets to share from that green thumb of yours?"

Scott chuckled, shaking his head in amusement. "Just the usual, Mrs. Jenkins," he replied. "Watering, weeding, and whispering sweet nothings to my plants."

Mrs. Jenkins let out a hearty laugh, her eyes twinkling with mirth. "Well, you must be quite the charmer then, Scott!" she exclaimed. "I've never seen a garden as lovely as yours."

As the days turned into weeks, Scott's garden flourished under his tender care, bursting with vibrant colors and intoxicating scents. But it wasn't just his plants that thrived—Scott's heart bloomed with love and laughter, too, thanks to an unexpected visitor who had wandered into his life.

One afternoon, as Scott was busy pruning his roses, he felt a gentle nudge against his leg. Looking down, he was met with the curious gaze of a stray cat—a scruffy little thing with fur as black as midnight and eyes as bright as the stars.

"Well, hello there, little one," Scott said, his heart melting at the sight of the furry intruder. "What brings you to my humble abode?"

To his surprise, the cat meowed in response, as if understanding every word he said. Scott couldn't help but laugh at the absurdity of the situation—here he was, having a conversation with a stray cat in his garden!

From that day on, the stray cat—whom Scott affectionately named Whiskers—became a regular visitor to his garden, keeping him company as he tended to his plants. Together, they would while away the hours, sharing stories and laughter amidst the beauty of nature.

And as Scott watched Whiskers darting playfully among the flowers, he couldn't help but feel a profound sense of gratitude for the unexpected joy that had entered his life. For in the laughter of a stray cat, he had found a kindred spirit—a companion to share his days with, in sickness and in health.

And so, dear reader, let Scott's story serve as a reminder that love knows no bounds, and that sometimes, laughter can be found in the most unexpected of places—even in the company of a stray cat in a humble garden.

Jack's Unexpected Visitor

In a quiet neighborhood where the streets hummed with the gentle rhythm of life, there lived a retired policeman named Jack. At seventy-six, Jack was known for his gruff exterior and no-nonsense demeanor, but beneath his tough exterior beat a heart full of love—a love that he had never quite learned how to express.

One crisp autumn morning, as Jack sipped his coffee and watched the world go by from his front porch, he received an unexpected visitor—a tiny kitten with eyes as bright as emeralds and a meow as soft as a whisper.

At first, Jack was reluctant to let the stray kitten into his home. After all, he was a retired policeman, not a cat whisperer. But as he looked into the kitten's pleading eyes, he felt something stir within him—a flicker of compassion that he couldn't ignore.

With a sigh, Jack scooped up the kitten in his arms and carried her inside, where he set about making her a makeshift bed out of an old cardboard box and a soft blanket. As he watched her curl up contentedly in her new bed, he couldn't help but feel a warmth spreading through his chest—a warmth that he hadn't felt in years.

In the days that followed, Jack found himself drawn to the kitten's side, his gruff exterior melting away with each playful swat of her tiny paw and each affectionate purr. Before long, he found himself talking to her as if she were an old friend, sharing stories of his days on the force and his hopes and dreams for the future.

As weeks turned into months, Jack and the kitten forged a bond that was as unbreakable as it was unexpected. She became his constant companion, his confidante, and his source of comfort in times of need.

But it wasn't just the kitten who had captured Jack's heart—it was the love that she brought into his life. With each passing day, he found himself opening up more and more, allowing himself to feel emotions that he had long kept buried beneath his tough exterior.

And as he watched the sunset from his front porch, with the kitten purring contentedly in his lap, Jack realized that love came in many forms. It wasn't just about romantic love or love for family—it was about the simple acts of kindness and compassion that brought joy and meaning to our lives.

In the arms of his newfound furry friend, Jack found a love that was pure and unconditional—a love that had the power to heal old wounds and ignite new passions. And as he drifted off to sleep that night, with the kitten curled up beside him, he knew that he was truly blessed to have found love in the most unexpected of places.

Grandpa James' Secret Love

Once upon a time, in a cozy little house nestled on the outskirts of town, there lived a wise old man named Grandpa James. He was a man of many stories, but there was one tale he had never shared with anyone—until one fateful day when his grandchildren, Jane and Jimmy, came to visit.

As they gathered around the fireplace, Jane and Jimmy begged their grandfather to tell them a story they had never heard before. And so, with a twinkle in his eye and a smile on his lips, Grandpa James began to recount the tale of his first love.

"It all started many years ago, when I was just a young lad," Grandpa James began, his voice filled with nostalgia. "Her name was Diana—a dark-haired beauty with eyes as green as emeralds. From the moment I first laid eyes on her, I knew she was something special."

Grandpa James regaled his grandchildren with tales of his adventures with Diana, from picnics in the park to long walks along the riverbank. He spoke of the laughter they shared, the secrets they whispered, and the butterflies that fluttered in his stomach whenever she was near.

"But you see, children, there was a problem," Grandpa James continued, his voice tinged with regret. "I was too afraid to tell Diana how I felt. I was scared of rejection, scared of ruining our friendship. So, I kept my feelings hidden away, locked up tight in my heart."

Jane and Jimmy listened intently, hanging on their grandfather's every word as he recounted the tale of his lost love. They could see the sadness in his eyes, the weight of regret that lingered in his soul.

"But you know what, children?" Grandpa James said, his voice growing stronger with each word. "Looking back now, I realize that love is worth taking a chance on. It's worth risking your heart for, even if it means facing rejection or disappointment."

Grandpa James smiled warmly at his grandchildren, a twinkle of mischief dancing in his eyes. "And you know what else? I may have never told Diana how I felt, but I did find the courage to tell another special someone—a woman named Mary, who stole my heart and became my beloved wife."

Jane and Jimmy gasped in surprise, their eyes widening with wonder. They had never heard this part of their grandfather's story before, and they couldn't help but feel a surge of love and admiration for the man who had shared his deepest secrets with them.

As they cuddled closer to their grandfather, Jane and Jimmy realized that love was not just about grand gestures or sweeping romances—it was about the little moments, the shared laughter, and the courage to be vulnerable.

And as they sat together by the fire, surrounded by warmth and love, they knew that they would always cherish the tale of Grandpa James' secret love—a story that reminded them to seize every opportunity, cherish every moment, and never be afraid to follow their hearts.

Love Across the Tracks – A True Story

In the bustling city of Bologna, where the ancient streets echoed with the whispers of history, a young student named Carolina boarded a train bound for Florence. She had a sparkle in her eyes and a smile on her lips, eager to explore the world beyond the confines of her university.

Little did she know, her life was about to change forever.

Across the compartment sat Massimiliano, a dashing executive traveling for work. As their eyes met, sparks flew, and soon they were deep in conversation, sharing laughs and stories as the train sped through the Italian countryside.

Hours passed like minutes, and before they knew it, they had arrived at Carolina's stop. With a twinkle in her eye, she bid Massimiliano farewell, leaving him with a lingering sense of longing.

But as she disappeared into the crowd, Massimiliano realized his mistake—he had never asked for her surname or telephone number.

Years passed, and Massimiliano often found himself haunted by the memory of the girl on the train. He married, as was expected of him, and built a life with his work colleague, but deep down, he knew that his heart belonged to another.

Meanwhile, Carolina's life took a different path. Despite her best efforts, she never found the right man, and as the years went by, she resigned herself to a life of solitude.

But fate works in mysterious ways, and sometimes, it has a way of bringing people back together.

One fateful day, at the age of seventy-five, Massimiliano found himself once again aboard a train, his heart heavy with memories of the past. As he settled into his seat, he couldn't shake the feeling that something extraordinary was about to happen.

And then, he saw her—the woman in the compartment next to his, her eyes sparkling with recognition as she caught sight of him. Without hesitation, Massimiliano approached her, his heart pounding with anticipation.

"Carolina?" he asked, his voice barely above a whisper.

And in that moment, time seemed to stand still as the two lost souls found each other once again.
Their reunion was like something out of a fairytale—full of laughter and tears, joy and disbelief. As they shared stories of their lives apart, they realized that their connection had never truly faded, despite the passing years.

And so, they made a decision—a decision to follow their hearts and pursue the love that had eluded them for so long.

For Massimiliano, it meant leaving behind the woman he had never truly loved, to be with the one who had captured his heart all those years ago.

And for Carolina, it meant taking a chance on love once again, even after so many disappointments.

Together, they embarked on a new journey—a journey filled with hope and possibility, guided by the timeless power of love.

And as they walked hand in hand into the sunset, their hearts full to bursting with happiness, they knew that they had finally found their happily ever after.

SERENITY

Welcome to the tranquil oasis of "Serenity" within the pages of "Cheery Uplifting Short Stories for Seniors" by Margaret Rivers—a collection crafted to envelop readers in a cocoon of peace, tranquility, and profound calm.

In the bustling tapestry of life, serenity stands as a beacon of solace, offering respite from the chaos and noise of the world. For seniors over 70, in particular, cultivating a sense of serenity becomes increasingly vital, serving as a sanctuary for the mind, body, and spirit amidst the ebb and flow of daily existence.

In this section, we embark on a soul-stirring journey through landscapes of boundless beauty and vistas of profound serenity. From the tranquil majesty of rolling hills to the gentle lullaby of ocean waves, each story is a testament to the transformative power of serenity—a force that soothes the soul, calms the mind, and nourishes the spirit.

As the sun sets on another day, these stories beckon readers to immerse themselves in moments of quiet reflection and inner peace. Through Margaret Rivers' evocative prose, readers are transported to idyllic locales where time seems to stand still, and worries melt away in the embrace of nature's embrace.

At the heart of this section lies the enchantment of a sunset—a symbol of transition, renewal, and the promise of a new beginning. As readers gaze upon the canvas of the sky painted in hues of gold, crimson, and indigo, they are reminded of life's inherent beauty and the cyclical nature of existence.

But beyond the physical landscapes, the stories within this section also explore the inner landscapes of the human heart, where serenity resides as a quiet, steadfast companion. Through moments of introspection and self-discovery, characters find solace in the stillness of their own thoughts, learning to embrace the present moment with grace and acceptance.

From the gentle rustle of leaves in a forest glade to the hushed whispers of a mountain stream, each story is a symphony of serenity—an invitation to pause, breathe, and connect with the timeless rhythms of the natural world.

As you journey through these tales of tranquility, may you find solace in the beauty of the present moment, and may you discover the power of serenity to restore, renew, and rejuvenate the soul. For in the quiet spaces between the words, lies the essence of serenity—a gift to be cherished, savored, and shared with others.

These stories are more than mere words on a page; they are portals to a realm of inner peace and tranquility—a sanctuary for the weary traveler seeking refuge from the storms of life. Whether enjoyed alone in the stillness of the night or shared with loved ones as bedtime stories, may these tales of serenity serve as a gentle reminder that amidst life's trials and tribulations, there is always a place of calm and quiet waiting to be discovered.

So let us embark on this journey together, guided by the gentle whispers of the wind and the soft glow of the moon, as we surrender to the embrace of serenity and allow its healing touch to envelop us in its warm embrace.

Mildred's Misadventures at the Senior Center

In the quaint town of Willowbrook, where the days drifted lazily like leaves on a gentle breeze, there lived a retired hairdresser named Mildred. At seventy-eight, Mildred was known for her sharp wit, her love of laughter, and her penchant for getting into hilarious mishaps.

One bright Tuesday morning, Mildred decided to pay a visit to the local senior center. With her trusty pair of scissors tucked into her purse and a mischievous twinkle in her eye, she set off on what promised to be a day filled with serenity, laughter, and perhaps a little bit of trouble.

As Mildred strolled through the doors of the senior center, she was greeted with warm smiles and hearty hellos from her fellow residents. With a flourish, she produced her scissors and announced that she was offering free haircuts to anyone brave enough to take a chance on her skills.

Before long, Mildred found herself surrounded by eager volunteers, each clamoring for a chance to sit in her makeshift salon chair. With a wink and a grin, she set to work, her scissors dancing through the air with practiced ease.

But Mildred's haircuts were no ordinary affairs. Oh no, they were wild and whimsical creations, each one more outrageous than the last. From mohawks to mullets, buzz cuts to bouffants, Mildred's salon became a riot of laughter and lighthearted fun.

As the day wore on, Mildred's mischievous streak got the better of her, and she decided to spice things up a bit. With a twinkle in her eye and a giggle in her heart, she began to experiment with bold new styles and daring hair colors, much to the delight (and horror) of her unsuspecting clients.

Before long, the senior center was abuzz with laughter and excitement as Mildred unveiled her latest masterpieces. There were gasps of surprise and peals of laughter as residents admired each other's wild new looks, and Mildred basked in the glow of her newfound fame.

But Mildred's adventures didn't end there. As the day drew to a close, she found herself caught up in a spirited game of bingo, where her quick wit and sharp tongue earned her a few good-natured groans and plenty of belly laughs.

And as the sun dipped below the horizon and the laughter faded into the night, Mildred realized that sometimes, the best adventures are the ones that find you when you least expect them. With a contented sigh and a smile on her face, she bid her friends farewell and headed home, her heart full of laughter and her spirit soaring with serenity.

The Healing Humor of Dr. Grace

In the quaint town of Willowbrook, where the days sauntered by like leisurely strolls in the park, there lived an elderly pharmacist named Alfred. At eighty-three, Alfred had spent a lifetime dispensing pills and potions to the good folks of the town, but there was one thing he had never confessed to anyone—he was terrified of doctors.

Despite his fear, Alfred's advancing age eventually led him to the doors of the local hospital. As he lay in his hospital bed, surrounded by beeping machines and bustling nurses, his heart raced with anxiety. But little did he know that his fears were about to be assuaged by an unexpected source—Dr. Grace, the hospital's newest recruit.

With her bright smile and gentle demeanor, Dr. Grace was a breath of fresh air in the sterile corridors of the hospital. As she bustled about, checking on patients and doling out words of encouragement, Alfred couldn't help but feel a sense of calm wash over him in her presence.

But it wasn't just Dr. Grace's professional demeanor that put Alfred at ease—it was her sense of humor. With a quick wit and a playful twinkle in her eye, she had a knack for turning even the most serious of situations into moments of levity and laughter.

One afternoon, as Dr. Grace made her rounds, she found Alfred staring nervously at the ceiling, his brow furrowed with worry. With a sympathetic smile, she pulled up a chair beside his bed and launched into a series of silly jokes and amusing anecdotes, each one more outrageous than the last.

Before long, Alfred found himself chuckling despite himself, his fears melting away like snow in the spring sunshine. As he laughed along with Dr. Grace, he realized that he had never felt more at ease in a hospital setting in his entire life.

From that day forward, Alfred looked forward to Dr. Grace's visits with eager anticipation. Her lighthearted banter and infectious laughter lifted his spirits and filled him with a sense of serenity that he had never thought possible in a hospital setting.

And as Alfred lay in his hospital bed, surrounded by the gentle hum of medical equipment and the comforting presence of Dr. Grace, he knew that he had overcome his lifelong fear of doctors. With her help, he had found the courage to face his fears head-on and emerge stronger and more resilient than ever before.

As he drifted off to sleep that night, a peaceful smile graced Alfred's lips, his heart full of gratitude for the young doctor who had brought him so much comfort and joy in his time of need. And in that moment, he realized that sometimes, laughter truly was the best medicine of all.

Sunset Serenity

In the bustling city where the pace of life never seemed to slow, there lived a recently retired business manager named Albert. At seventy-eight, Albert had spent a lifetime chasing success and climbing the corporate ladder, his days filled with meetings, deadlines, and endless stress.

But as Albert's retirement loomed on the horizon, he found himself gripped by a sense of anxiety and worthlessness. For so long, his identity had been tied to his career, and the thought of stepping into the unknown filled him with dread.

To make matters worse, Albert's wife, Lily, seemed to revel in the calm and serenity that he so desperately craved. Her laid-back attitude and passion for the simple pleasures in life—like watching the sunset over the sea—had always puzzled and even irritated Albert.

"Life is too short to waste it worrying," Lily would say with a smile, her eyes twinkling with mischief.

But as Albert's retirement approached, he began to see things in a new light. With each passing day, he found himself drawn to Lily's love for sunsets, her appreciation for the beauty and tranquility of the natural world.

And so, on the day of his retirement, Albert made a decision—he would embrace Lily's passion for sunsets and make it his own. Armed with a camera and a newfound sense of adventure, he set out on a journey across the country in search of the most beautiful sunsets to see and photograph.

From the rugged coastline of the north to the sun-kissed beaches of the south, Albert traveled far and wide, each sunset more breathtaking than the last. With each click of his camera, he felt a sense of peace wash over him— a serenity that he had never experienced in the boardroom.

But it wasn't just the beauty of the sunsets that filled Albert with joy—it was the time spent with Lily, sharing quiet moments together as they watched the sun dip below the horizon, painting the sky in a riot of colors.

As the days turned into weeks and the weeks turned into months, Albert's anxiety began to fade away, replaced by a sense of contentment and fulfillment that he had never known before. He realized that retirement wasn't about slowing down or stepping out of the spotlight—it was about embracing life's simple pleasures and finding joy in the little moments.

And so, as Albert and Lily watched the sunset from their favorite spot on the beach, their hands intertwined and their hearts full of love, he knew that he had finally found the serenity that he had been searching for all along. And as the last rays of sunlight faded into the night, Albert whispered a silent thank you to Lily for showing him the true meaning of life's most precious gift—peace of mind.

Reunited in Serenity

Margaret, an 82-year-old woman with a heart as resilient as an oak tree, had spent two decades carrying the weight of a rift between her and her brother, Charles. Their once-close relationship had soured over an inheritance dispute, leaving Margaret with a bitter taste in her mouth and a heavy burden on her heart.

It all started when their father passed away, leaving behind a piece of land with sentimental value to Margaret. But Charles, driven by greed and entitlement, had demanded a share of the inheritance through his lawyer, igniting a feud that tore their family apart.

For years, Margaret and Charles had avoided each other like the plague, their resentment festering like a wound that refused to heal. But deep down, Margaret longed for nothing more than to mend their fractured relationship and find peace in her heart once again.

One fateful day, Margaret received a call from the cemetery attendant, informing her that he needed to discuss the family chapel—an unexpected summons that would unknowingly set the stage for a long-awaited reconciliation. As Margaret made her way to the cemetery office, her mind raced with thoughts of the past and hopes for the future.

Meanwhile, across town, Charles received the same call from the cemetery attendant, his heart heavy with regret for the years lost to bitterness and resentment. As he made his way to the office, he couldn't shake the feeling that this meeting held the key to unlocking the serenity he so desperately craved.

When Margaret and Charles arrived at the cemetery office, they were greeted by the sight of each other—a sight that filled them both with a mix of surprise and apprehension. For a moment, they stood in awkward silence, the weight of their shared history hanging heavily in the air.

But as they sat down together, facing the cemetery attendant and the task at hand, something remarkable happened. With each passing moment, the walls that had long separated Margaret and Charles began to crumble, replaced by a newfound sense of understanding and empathy.

As they discussed the details of the family chapel and the responsibilities that came with it, Margaret and Charles found themselves opening up to each other in ways they never thought possible. They shared memories of their childhood, laughter over shared experiences, and tears over the pain they had inflicted on each other over the years.

And in that moment, surrounded by the quiet serenity of the cemetery office, Margaret and Charles realized that their bond was stronger than any dispute or disagreement. They embraced each other with tearful hugs, letting go of the past and embracing the promise of a brighter future together.

As they left the cemetery office hand in hand, Margaret and Charles felt a sense of peace wash over them like a gentle breeze. For in that moment of reconciliation, they had found not only closure but also the serenity that had eluded them for so long. And as they walked away together, their hearts light and their spirits lifted, they knew that nothing could ever come between them again.

A Lesson in Serenity

Oliver was a man of routine. As an elderly university professor with a stern demeanor, he approached life with a disciplined mindset, valuing logic and reason above all else. His days were meticulously planned, each hour accounted for in pursuit of scholarly endeavors.

But one fateful morning, as Oliver set out to buy his usual loaf of bread from the neighborhood bakery, he found himself drawn to a small gathering in the park. Curiosity piqued, he approached cautiously, his skepticism palpable.

What he discovered was a group of people engaged in a practice he had heard of but never paid much attention to: yoga. As he watched the gentle movements and heard the soft murmurs of the instructor guiding the participants through the poses, Oliver felt an unexpected sense of peace wash over him.

Intrigued, Oliver lingered on the outskirts of the group, observing with keen interest. When the session concluded, he approached the instructor—a serene woman named Maya—with a mixture of skepticism and curiosity.

"Yoga, is it?" he asked, his tone brimming with skepticism.

Maya smiled warmly, her eyes twinkling with kindness. "Yes, it is. Would you like to give it a try?"

Oliver hesitated, his rational mind warring with the flicker of curiosity within him. But something about Maya's gentle demeanor compelled him to nod his assent.

And so, Oliver found himself unrolling a yoga mat and attempting to mimic the poses he had observed moments earlier. At first, he stumbled and faltered, his movements awkward and stiff. But with Maya's patient guidance, he began to find a rhythm, his muscles gradually loosening with each stretch and twist.

As the session drew to a close, Oliver felt a sense of calm settle over him—a rare sensation for a man accustomed to the frenetic pace of academia. He realized that in the quiet moments between poses, there was a stillness he had long been missing—a serenity that seemed to elude him in his everyday life.

In the days that followed, Oliver found himself drawn back to the park, eager to immerse himself in the practice of yoga once more. With each session, he felt a profound shift within himself, as if layers of tension and stress were being peeled away to reveal the true essence of his being.

As he delved deeper into the practice, Oliver discovered a newfound sense of compassion and empathy blossoming within him. He found himself more patient with his students, more understanding of their struggles and fears. And in the quiet moments of meditation, he found solace in the simple act of being present—a gift he had long overlooked in his relentless pursuit of knowledge.

In the end, it wasn't just yoga that changed Oliver's life— it was the serenity and compassion it awakened within him. And as he moved through the world with a newfound sense of peace, he realized that sometimes, the greatest lessons are found in the most unexpected of places.

The Journey of Serenity

In a quaint neighborhood nestled between rolling hills and winding roads, lived Mary and Mark—a couple whose hearts were filled with wanderlust and a passion for adventure. Together, they had traversed the globe, exploring the vibrant capitals of Europe, the sun-kissed beaches of Mexico, and the enchanting landscapes of faraway lands.

Their most cherished memory? A night spent under the dazzling display of the Northern Lights in Lapland—a moment of serenity that seemed to stretch into eternity.

As retirement loomed on the horizon, Mark eagerly anticipated the prospect of embarking on even grander adventures with Mary by his side. They dreamt of traversing the globe in search of new sights and experiences, their hearts brimming with excitement.

But fate had other plans.

A nagging ear problem sidelined Mark's dreams of travel, grounding him indefinitely. For a man accustomed to a life of movement and exploration, the news was devastating.

Days turned into weeks, and Mark found himself grappling with a sense of restlessness and discontent. The thought of being confined to their home while the world beckoned beyond the horizon weighed heavily on his spirit.

But then, a glimmer of hope appeared on the horizon.

Joseph, their neighbor and fellow adventurer, unveiled his latest acquisition—a magnificent camper van that promised endless possibilities and boundless freedom.

Mark, who had always dismissed the idea of camper van travel as too rustic and impractical, found himself inexplicably drawn to Joseph's enthusiasm. As he stepped inside the cozy interior and listened to Joseph recount tales of starry nights by the sea and tranquil moments amidst nature, something stirred within him.

Perhaps, he thought, there was serenity to be found in the simplicity of life on the open road.

Inspired by Joseph's passion, Mark began to entertain the idea of embarking on a new adventure—one that would defy the limitations imposed by his ear problem and reclaim the spirit of exploration that had defined his life.

With Mary's support, Mark took the plunge and purchased his own camper van—a symbol of newfound freedom and possibility. Together, they mapped out a route that would take them on a journey across the United States, from the majestic peaks of the Rockies to the sun-drenched shores of California.

As they set off on their grand adventure, Mark felt a sense of peace and serenity wash over him. Gone were the worries and anxieties that had plagued him in recent weeks, replaced instead by a profound sense of contentment and joy.

Each day brought new discoveries and unexpected encounters—a hidden waterfall tucked away in the mountains, a cozy diner serving up homemade pies, a quiet campground nestled beneath a canopy of stars.

And through it all, Mark and Mary found themselves falling in love with the simple pleasures of life on the road—the freedom to chart their own course, the beauty of unspoiled landscapes, and the sense of connection forged with fellow travelers along the way.

As they watched the sun set over the horizon, casting a golden glow across the landscape, Mark couldn't help but feel grateful for the journey that had brought them to this moment—a journey fueled by love, serenity, and the promise of endless possibility. And as they drifted off to sleep beneath a blanket of stars, he knew that their greatest adventure was only just beginning.

CONCLUSIONS

Through the exploration of five powerful positive emotions—hope, gratitude, love, serenity, and motivation—we have embarked on a journey of the heart, mind, and soul, guided by the gentle hand of author Margaret Rivers.

At the heart of this collection lies the profound truth that positive emotions are not only beneficial for our well-being but are essential for living a fulfilling and meaningful life.

Whether it's the hope that springs eternal in times of adversity, the gratitude that fills our hearts with joy and abundance, the love that binds us together in times of trial, the serenity that soothes our troubled minds, or the motivation and enthusiasm that propel us forward on our journey—the stories within these pages remind us of the inherent beauty and resilience of the human spirit. With each turn of the page, readers are invited to immerse themselves in stories that uplift the spirit, stimulate the mind, and evoke cherished memories of days gone by.

But perhaps the most remarkable aspect of this collection is its versatility. Designed to be read and re-read, savored and cherished, each story offers something unique to the reader depending on their mood, circumstance, and state of mind.

In times of sadness or despair, one can turn to the stories of motivation and enthusiasm, finding inspiration and courage to face life's challenges head-on. When feeling overwhelmed or anxious, the serene landscapes and calming narratives of the "serenity" section provide a much-needed respite from the chaos of the world. And in moments of reflection and gratitude, the tales of love, hope, and trust serve as a gentle reminder of life's blessings and miracles.

As we bid farewell to these uplifting tales, let us carry with us the lessons learned and the memories shared, knowing that within the pages of this book lies a source of comfort, joy, and inspiration for years to come. May it serve as a constant companion on life's journey, offering solace in times of sorrow, companionship in times of loneliness, and hope in times of despair.

And so, as we turn the final page and close the book on this chapter of our lives, let us embrace the beauty of the present moment and the infinite possibilities that lie ahead. For in the end, it is not the destination that matters, but the journey itself—the stories we tell, the memories we create, and the love we share along the way.

Thank you for allowing me the privilege of sharing these uplifting tales with you. May they continue to inspire, uplift, and instill positive emotions in your heart for years to come.

With warmest regards,
Margaret Rivers

Dear Reader,

As you close the book and return to the world outside its pages, I invite you to stay in touch. Whether you have requests, suggestions, comments, or simply want to share your thoughts and curiosities, please don't hesitate to reach out to me at **margaretriverswriter@gmail.com.**

Your feedback is invaluable to me, and it will help shape future editions of this book, ensuring that they are even better and more uplifting than before.

Additionally, if you have a moment to spare, <u>I would be incredibly grateful if you could take the time to write a <u>review of this book on Amazon.</u> Your honest feedback will not only help other readers discover these cheery stories but will also support and encourage me as I continue to pursue my passion for writing.

Once again, thank you from the bottom of my heart for joining me on this journey. May these stories continue to bring you joy, comfort, and inspiration for many years to come.

With warmest regards,

Printed in Great Britain
by Amazon